Just Country Gardens

by
Judy Condon

Library of Congress Cataloging-in-Publications Data
Just Country Gardens by Judy Condon
ISBN 978-0-9847028-0-0

Oceanic Graphic Printing, Inc.
105 Main Street
Hackensack, NJ 07601

Printed in China

Layout and Design by Pat Lucas
Edited by Trent Michaels

Table of Contents

Introduction 5

The Coulter Gardens 6

The Powell Gardens 14

The Friend/Coogan Gardens 17

The Hayes Gardens 21

The D'Esopo Gardens 29

The Bailey Gardens 37

The Hveem Gardens 46

The Moulton/Lane Gardens 50

The McCord Gardens 55

The Riggs Gardens 60

The Cole/Davidson Gardens 65

The Glen Gardens 69

The Sterling Gardens 75

The Garafalo Gardens 81

The Lindberg/Nelson Gardens 89

The Davidian Gardens 95

The Aker Gardens 99

The Windle Gardens 106

The Burnett Gardens 119

The Littiken Gardens 126

The Przystas/Chojnowski Gardens 133

About the Author

Judy Condon is a native New Englander, which is evident in her decorating style and the type of antiques she collects and sells. Her real passion is 19thC authentic dry red or blue painted pieces. While Judy enjoyed a professional career as a teacher, Principal, and Superintendent of Schools in Connecticut, Judy's weekends were spent at her antique shop, *Marsh Homestead Country Antiques*, located in Litchfield, Connecticut.

When her husband, Jeff, was relocated to Virginia, Judy accepted an early retirement from education and concentrated her energy and passion for antiques into a fulltime business. Judy maintains a website, *www.marshhomesteadantiques.com* and has been a Power Seller on eBay® for over 13 years under the name "superct".

Judy and her husband Jeff recently returned to their roots in New England and have completed renovating a 19thC cape in Massachusetts. Their home was featured in one of Judy's previous books, *Back Home – Simply Country*. Judy has five children and five grandchildren and enjoys reading, golf, bridge, tennis, and volunteering in the educational system in St Maarten. Judy does her best to provide teaching materials and children's books to the schools in St. Maarten with the hope of helping establish classroom libraries.

Judy's first 18 books in the "simply country" series, *Country on a Shoestring, Of Hearth and Home – Simply Country, A Simpler Time, Country Decorating for All Seasons, As Time Goes By, Country at Heart, Welcome Home – Simply Country, Home Again – Simply Country, The Warmth of Home, The Country Home, Simple Greens – Simply Country, The Country Life, Simply Country Gardens, The Spirit of Country, The Joy of Country, Holidays at a Country Home, A Touch of Country*, and *Back Home – Simply Country* have been instant hits and most are in their second printing. Judy may be reached through her Website *www.marshhomesteadantiques.com*, by email at *marshhomestead@comcast.net*, or by phone at 877-381-6682.

Introduction

I have a confession! I am a flower junkie. I admit it without shame and will go so far as to disclose that it is with great restraint that I pass by a garden center during flower planting season and don't stop. Actually, it doesn't happen often!

For years, I smuggled flats of potted flowers into my barn where they remained hidden until I could plant them inconspicuously . . . as though they had been there for months. Whatever made me think I was getting away with something is beyond me, as my diligent husband always checks each line item on the credit card bill–and what else would I have been purchasing from XYZ Nursery! I'm not sure which of us has had the last laugh; he who paid the bill each month without questioning the item, or me who miraculously filled garden beds overnight with mature plantings thinking that he hadn't noticed.

Having lived in Virginia nine years and struggling to create a garden in brick red clay soil and intense heat, I anxiously awaited spring planting season in our newly renovated 1825 cape in New England, featured in my last book, *Back Home*. With endless days of New England

spring rain, I eventually gave up waiting for sunshine and the man I'd hired to dig beds for me; I plunged in with the help of my husband, Jeff. Recognizing that next year I would be a year older, I began with only three beds, albeit rather large ones. I once again found myself stockpiling flats of plants behind the house and closely monitored the activities of a resident woodchuck– who probably thought he had died and gone to heaven with fresh meals so close at hand. I even felt obligated to advise the nursery that I knew they were enjoying a banner sales year and that perhaps they should not base next year's sales or inventory commitments on current volume. When two of my young grandchildren visited in August, imagine my delight when Chaz and JD asked if they could plant some flowers with me. Darn . . . another trip to the garden center!

Although I've lost some plants due to a hot and dry summer, most have survived. Already I'm looking ahead to next year, when roots will strengthen and stalks will grow straighter as a result of a stronger root base. My yarrow should stand up stronger, my liatris should feature stems that don't meander upward in a crooked path, and my bee balm will display a fuller bush.

I feel those of us who love gardening and flowers carry the passion in our blood. Our gardens bring us joy, as I never tire of the bed I planted outside my office window; I glance out and smile at the textures and colors "painted" against an old stone wall as a backdrop. Already I look forward to next season–to not only welcome back last year's beauties but also itch for the first sign that the nursery is open–and once more wonder how the heck I ended up in their parking lot. AGAIN!

Chapter 1

The Coulter Gardens

Glenn Coulter, a retired engineer, and his wife Dale, a nurse in an alcohol and drug detox facility are both originally from Sutton, Massachusetts, and were high school sweethearts. They purchased their 1798 home and moved in during the blizzard of 1978. In 2000, Dale attended her first garden tour in town and at the time kept only a vegetable garden surrounded by a ring of flowers. When Glenn and Dale decided to build a pool, the optimum spot proved to be the vegetable garden's location. Losing the family vote, Dale began to move her plants to other areas. Dale joined the Sutton Garden Club and was encouraged to include her own home on the following year's house tour– a daunting task since Dale had no flower gardens to speak of. While sitting in the Keeping Room that February, Dale began to imagine her gardens and drew up plans . . . the best part of gardening, according to Dale.

Dale had toured Longwood Gardens and noted a strategically placed pergola at an angle. She described the structure as one to "spiral 'round in a quarter circle". Glenn, who initially said, "What's a pergola?", proceeded to build a section at a time while Dale was at work. Their daughter has said she would like to be married under the finished "stage".

Dale and Glenn have a circle of friends who were each restoring early homes. They pooled their talent, time, and labor to complete each project; the gazebo beside the Coulter home was one such "circle of friends" undertaking.

The changing room beside the pool is decorated in keeping with the gardens and country setting.

When Dale and Glenn's son was younger, he raised chickens in the shed located beside the koi pool seen on the top of page 9. The shed was relocated on logs, bleached inside, and repurposed into a garden shed.

An out building, referred to as the garden house, is used for entertaining and provides a large space where Glenn and Dale practice their ballroom steps.

The area closest to the house in the back is filled with early blooming plants such as daffodils, iris, and hyacinths. Dale designed the area to appear and announce that spring has arrived and she could enjoy the gardens from the back windows.

She also plants a variety of herbs in these gardens, close to the back door.

Originally built as a woodshed when Glenn and Dale heated the house with wood, the shed has been converted into an ideal potting area.

The stump of a large 275 year-old diseased ash tree, nearly 54' in diameter and taken down by the town at the front of the house, became the focal point of a "friendship" garden in an area formerly used for parking.

Dale and Glenn thought they would use the disks cut from the stump to make tables, but then decided to be creative and design what is now the lily garden, which suddenly appeared in Dale's driveway.

The children's two-room playhouse is decorated inside with a punched tin chandelier and an oriental rug; it rests alongside the lily garden and has been dressed up with whimsical, tin daisies.

Dale sometimes spends an entire day off working in her gardens. Many evenings, Dale relieves the pressure of her rewarding but extremely stressful work day by weeding her gardens. The entire area is lighted, and, as she said, "I can weed until midnight if I need it."

Chapter 2

The Powell Gardens

Leslie and Steve Powell's home was featured in *A Touch of Country*, but the few garden pictures did not do justice to the property. They purchased their 1777 home in Bantam, Connecticut, 13 years ago and immediately opened *Toll House Antiques*, seen above and located just a hop and skip over the babbling brook which separates the house and the shop.

Leslie wanted to capture the essence of a period garden and had a friend create the layout and raised beds. A single birdhouse in the center, purchased at *White Flower Farm* in Litchfield, Connecticut, provides a focal point. A hooded shelf, made by a local artisan, holds a bee skep and is a popular seller in Leslie's shop.

The stone wall shown below was built with stones found on the property.

A walking bridge, the design taken from a bridge in my first garden book, Simply Country Gardens, provides a crossover for the brook leading from the main pond.

Leslie's shop is open by appointment only. The phone number for Toll House Antiques is 860-567-3130.

Chapter 3

❦ ✵ ❦

The Friend/Coogan Gardens

Elizabeth Jane Friend and her husband, James Coogan live in Sandwich, Massachusetts, in a house built by Samuel Fessenden in 1840. He worked for the Boston/Sandwich Glass Company, which put Sandwich on the map. Elizabeth Jane, an art historian, teaches a course in American folk art at the Cape Cod Community College. When she isn't teaching or maintaining space for her business, *Mariah's Folk*, at the Seaside Antiques Shop, she is expanding her gardens which surround their home. Elizabeth Jane takes advantage of Cape Cod's soil and finds that certain plants, such as hydrangea, thrive in the sandy loam. She plants varieties which thrive during the warm summers and plentiful rainfall the Cape offers.

Elizabeth Jane feels she owes much of her education and success in the garden to a nearby garden center, *Olsen's Nursery*. Her husband, James, is a published author of both children's and adult books on Cape Cod history. His most recent book, *Clarence The Cranberry Who Couldn't Bounce*, is available from Harvest Home Books and may be ordered by calling 508-833-2952.

Elizabeth Jane uses a variety of impatiens throughout the yard as they thrive in the shaded areas.

Seen at the back of the house is an outdoor shower, which Elizabeth Jane reports is common on Cape Cod and its use in the summer a custom for Cape Cod residents.

Elizabeth Jane reports that they spend their warm summer evenings enjoying the screened porch at the back of the garage. Potted impatiens surround the area, thriving in the limited sunlight.

An area in the back is set aside as a tribute to three of the Coogan's dogs.

Chapter 4

The Hayes Gardens

Steve and Laurie Hayes purchased their 1739 colonial located in Cotuit, Massachusetts, in 1991. The property consists of approximately two acres of land, most of which features plants and flowers. Steve operates the *Sow's Ear Antique Company* from their home and takes care of the heavy lifting, while Laurie, a mortgage banker, maintains the flower beds.

Their home will be featured in a book next year. Steve admits that their gardens have gotten a bit out of hand and that they seem to have "created a monster". Using antique pieces, birdhouses, and a Cape Cod flair in their gardens, he reported that they more or less "make it up as they go along". The result is remarkable. The *Sow's Ear Antique Co.* is open year-round 10-4 and is located at 4698 Falmouth Road in Cotuit.

Steve used his skills as a former dock builder to create the pergola on the back patio.

A recent addition to the landscape is a
clambake pit, which Steve reports is used
throughout the summer.

Shorebirds can be seen perched on posts and
fences throughout the gardens on page 25.

The Hayes Gardens 27

One of the outbuildings serves as the garden shop. Here Steve sells a combination of old and new lawn and garden pieces.

Chapter 5

The D'Esopo Gardens

When Chrissie and John D'Esopo first saw the 1760's property in Avon, Connecticut that they would end up calling home, the house was in serious disrepair without plumbing, electricity, or heat. Despite the fact that there were no stairs to the second floor and the D'Esopos had no idea what the upstairs looked like, they bought the house. John, a general contractor, totally restored the home within three months. Chrissie, who works as an independent decorative home painter and consultant, spends eight hours a day watering the more than 900 clay-filled pots of annuals. In early spring, Chrissie has been known to work 15 hours a day for over a week to plant nearly 20,000 plants in the beds surrounding the house, including large urns and planters.

Chrissie loves to collect starfish and uses them to adorn the shutters and front door wreath with a seascape theme.

Chrissie's creativity and passion for the unusual takes form in the 10-foot long dragon she designed using chicken wire, sphagnum moss, and grow mix. She fashioned the dragon's claws and teeth from clay.

A starfish tops the roof above the cathedral window of the three-bay Greek Revival barn in back.

A collection of early tools and farm equipment is displayed on the barn board surrounding the back entrance to the house.

A steep hillside creates a large palette for bursts of color. Using tree stumps to hold some of the over 300 planters, Chrissie adds depth and height to the space.

A cascading waterfall feeds a pond filled with koi and carp.

Chapter 6
❧ ✿ ❧
The Bailey Gardens

Bob, retired from a 20-year career in the marine and retail merchant business, and his wife Elsie, retired from a primitive antique business for 25 years, now have time to devote to their gardens and home. Elsie and Bob built their Lebanon, Missouri home in 1975 and have continued to make changes since the day they moved in. Even after 56 years of married life, they haven't slowed down. Their delightful garden house, seen at the end of the chapter, was just added last year. Future plans include adding a picket fence and creating another garden area connected to the garden house. As Elsie said, "Every year we have a new project to make it better." They also find time to enjoy two children, four grandsons, and four great-grandchildren.

Chapter 7

The Hveem Gardens

Susan Hveem and her late husband Harvey purchased their 1790 Woodbury, Connecticut home 10 years ago when the backyard featured eight 25' hemlocks and 37 trees in the front yard alone. Taking the first few years to design the patio with steps and create stone walls, Susan and Harvey then cleared the hemlocks and were able to see the back of their property for the first time. Removing all the trees in front created a lovely lawn (now mostly flowers) surrounded by stone walls they built themselves. Susan can look out any window and see her gardens, which include 45 plants she brought from their previous home. She strategically places her plants so that something blooms in each bed every month. Through experimentation, Susan has found that mulching with fish soil has been a sure way to help her gardens thrive.

Among the annuals in her large bed near the back door, Susan includes some of Harvey's grandmother's peonies, which Susan has taken with her each time she and Harvey moved over the years.

Susan's home is filled with lovely antiques and the reader can tour the interior in a future book. She views her garden additions in the same way she does her antiques; each tree and country accessory carries with it a memory of where it was purchased or a special occasion she shared with Harvey.

Harvey was an avid pigeon flyer and owned a number of rare homing pigeons. Because of his hobby, Susan purchases various pigeon collectibles in her travels; one such example is the concrete pigeon on the cement stand, seen above.

The Hveem Gardens 49

Chapter 8

⌢ ✿ ⌢

The Moulton/Carpenter Gardens

As long as Mark Kimball Moulton and Lane Carpenter are willing to keep moving and refurbishing homes, I'm willing to keep photographing them and including their works of art in my books! This is the third home that Mark and Lane have redone since I've known them and I jumped at the opportunity to include their gardens. The interior of their home will be included in a future house tour book.

Author and photographer Mark Kimball Moulton and his partner Lane Carpenter purchased their early 1900's home in central Connecticut in 2009 and immediately began total renovation, including an addition off the back. Utilizing a talented builder who Mark prefers to call an artist, and a barn full of reclaimed materials, Sparrowood of Avon became a reality.

Mark's degree in horticulture proved invaluable as he designed several theme gardens and intimate "garden rooms" throughout the property. Mark painstakingly transported mature shrubs and perennials from his former home affording the new beds an instant, established look.

Mark and Lane placed country accessories throughout the grounds to offer a hint of what to expect on the inside.

Sparrowood is located in a charming, old-world neighborhood of well-kept vintage homes, where gardens bloom alongside sidewalks and block parties or movie nights are a common occurrence.

A short distance off the front porch, a multitude of fine restaurants and quaint shops are within easy walking distance. A stroll to the left leads to hiking trails and an expansive nature preserve. There's even a slow moving river and a Huckleberry Finn-like bridge, rope swing, and lazy day swimming hole.

To learn more about Mark and
his work, please visit his website at
www.MarkKimballMoulton.com.

Chapter 9

The McCord Gardens

Janice and Phil McCord became instant heroes in the neighborhood when they purchased their Greenfield, Indiana, 1850's eyesore home just before it was to be bulldozed! At the time, the property was overgrown with brush-and one large boulder on each corner served as the foundation holding the house in place. Phil and Janice immediately began to clear the brush, incorporate the boulders into their flower beds, and create simple, informal gardens in the back. Janice wanted to replicate the home's unpretentious and serene feeling into her gardens, as well.

Janice loves displaying fresh cut flowers in the house throughout the summer; she makes sure to plant enough flowers to fill vases in each room.

Janice and Phil are always looking for unusual plants that will attract birds and butterflies. Throughout the yard, there are numerous bushes and trees that produce winter berries for birds.

When Janice isn't working in her gardens, she can be found at her shop, The Red Rooster, located at 1001 W. Main Street in Greenfield. She is open Monday–Saturday year-round from 10-5. Janice can be reached at 317-462-0655 or her email theredrooster@hrtc.net.

Janice enjoys changing the theme in their screened porch and has been known to decorate it with a Hawaiian theme on occasion.

Chapter 10

The Riggs Gardens

Carol and Steve Riggs built their center chimney colonial in 1999 on land that had been in their family since 1863. Their property, located in Marshall, Michigan, is recognized as a centennial property-meaning it has been owned by the same family for over 100 years.

The house is surrounded by fields which are rented out to tenants for corn and soy beans. When Carol and Steve built the house, they paid particular attention to its positioning so that windows would provide a spectacular view from any spot in the house.

Carol was able to finally convince their builder that she wanted "simple". Her gated gardens in front resemble those she had seen when visiting Colonial Williamsburg; her goal was to create gardens with a New England look.

Carol used pea stone in her front gardens as she wanted to create a contrast with the back gardens which are bricked.

For a recent garden tour, Carol placed a fresh pineapple on each post which added a unique touch and a fresh aroma.

Carol believes the beauty of a garden is not singly in the colors and textures of the flowers but the country pieces which are added to the space. Two pineapple finials, for example, on the primitive bench provide a backdrop for the surrounding plants.

An early wagon is filled with a single potted petunia fertilized with Miracle Gro!

A friend made the small outbuilding which Carol uses to hold garden equipment; it also provides another display space.

The shed with the shutters came from a neighboring property and was formerly an outhouse. Carol approached the neighbor and asked if she could purchase the building. The owner told her she couldn't purchase it but she could have it. Steve added the wooden shakes roof.

Carol remembers visiting the farm when she was a young girl and watching her grandmother work in her garden. However, with almost 30 years experience, Carol credits her sister as having inspired her the most.

Chapter 11

❧ ✿ ❧

The Cole/Davidson Gardens

When Melinda Cole and her mother Winifred Davidson each sadly lost their husbands within four months of each other, Melinda and her high school aged son, Evan, decided to move into Winifred's home and share her 1810 Tipp City, Ohio house. The house, a federal farmhouse, was built by Quakers and rests on 15 acres where they grow hay and soy beans. In addition to farming, Melinda and her mother adopt retired race horses and currently own two. Melinda enjoys rug hooking, stitching samplers, and quilting when not busy in the gardens beside her mother. Winifred, a former artist and musician, started gardening over 50 years ago; Melinda attributes all she knows about the subject to her mother.

The barn behind the house is called a bank barn and is original to the property; it is built into a hillside with an opening on one side for animals to walk in and out. The hillside construction provides cool temps in the summer and warmth in the winter.

The quaint potting shed is the original milk house. A concrete surface on one side holds potted plants and conceals a space below; Melinda believes the space was perhaps used by the Underground Railroad.

The gardens are a joint effort; both Melinda and Winifred like to see color throughout the growing season and try to plant so that something is in bloom at all times. They also plant annuals for sustaining color and use pots to do so. As Melinda admitted, using pots allows the flexibility to place the pot on a stand until the plant grows taller and the stand can be removed. It also allows the freedom to rearrange parts of the garden as the summer passes.

I like the variety of plants with different tones of green in the garden . . . dark green to clusters of brighter green to the blue/green tones of the lavender. Melinda and Winifred use boxwoods to sustain interest in the winter and refer to them as the "bones of the garden".

Melinda likes to enhance her gardens with buckets, birdhouses, and even an old floral wastebasket belonging to her grandmother. What a great idea!

Chapter 12

❦ ◈ ❦

The Glen Gardens

Ron Glen, a regional VP for a facilities management company and his wife Linda love to landscape and garden. However, Linda admits that she chooses the plants, shows Ron where to plant them and he digs the holes. They have done all the landscaping themselves around their Northampton, Pennsylvania home. When Linda is not working in her garden or working on the inside of her home, she works as an assistant buyer at wholesale trade shows with Affordable Interiors by Fay. In the early 1990's, when her daughters Lindsay and Brittany were toddlers, Linda made country dolls so she could stay at home with the girls. However, she found she couldn't keep up with the orders and take care of the children, too, so she had to give up her doll making. Now she channels her creative talents making holiday arrangements which she sells at local craft shows. She also decided this year to make all her floral hanging baskets and large potted arrangements herself, which afforded her more opportunity to mix colors and varieties in her gardens.

The gazebo, deck, and patio were built almost 10 years prior to the in-ground pool; Linda and Ron worked successfully to incorporate the pool with the existing landscape.

The gazebo holds a set of wicker furniture; Linda has placed primitive accents among her tables and benches.

To the right of the frog, a pile of boulders creates a waterfall. Linda and Ron visited a quarry and handpicked all the boulders surrounding the pools; Linda wanted to give the area a rustic look. When the waterfall was under construction, Ron had to stand in the water supporting the boulders with PVC pipe while the contractor poured concrete to cement the boulders in place.

Linda has created a series of secluded seating areas around the pool deck and in the landscaped gardens.

A fireplace is a focal point in one sitting area. The lattice backboard conceals a bar area on the other side.

Linda enjoys using country pieces in her decorating outside; the more primitive the better! Linda and Ron's house will be featured in a house tour book next year.

Chapter 13

The Sterling Gardens

Emma Jane Sterling was born on Tangier Island located 12 miles off the coast of Virginia. It is an island of 550 residents who speak their own dialect of Elizabethan English and who travel the island on golf carts and bikes. Although her family left Tangier when Emma Jane was a young girl, she retains a bit of her unique accent. Nick, now retired from the dealership he owned selling marine engines, and Emma Jane have over 50 animal "pets" they care for on their Marion, Maryland farm.

Emma Jane first saw plans for their home in an Early American Life magazine in 1979 and knew that if they ever moved, she wanted to build that house. Her wish came true. The house is peacefully located in the middle of farmland, and not another house can be seen with the naked eye. The interior of the Sterling's home is decorated in first period and will be featured in a future book.

The property was originally a gristmill and land records date to the mid 17thC. One small outbuilding is a 150 year-old milk house given to Emma Jane as a Christmas gift from Nick.

Much of the Sterling's backyard area is shaded and contains many hostas and lambs ear.

Emma Jane loves to putter in her gardens, although she admits it's a lot of hard work. She has always enjoyed "just getting down in the dirt" as she calls it and spends almost four hours each morning in the spring and summer tending her garden beds and animals, such as ducks, pheasants, and geese.

A secluded area patio out the back door was designed as a spot to sit and enjoy her beds, but Emma Jane admits that often she sits down only long enough to notice a bed that needs weeding or watering.

An old smokehouse, given to Emma Jane by the previous owner, becomes the focal point in a sectioned area by the side of the driveway.

Emma Jane selected Japanese boxwood because they grow quickly and she wanted to achieve a finished boxwood look in a hurry. She is now paying the price as the shrubs require trimming three times each season and, in hindsight, she wishes she had chosen English boxwood.

Chapter 14

❦ ✿ ❦

The Garofalo Gardens

Marylyn Garofalo, a native New Yorker, found her dream cape in the middle of Pennsylvania where stone homes and farmhouses are more the norm than a New England-style cape. The 1951 home was built by a couple from Cape Cod and was decorated in a typical 50's style. Marylyn, however, couldn't resist the house as it was situated on a double lot in the middle of a small community and close to everything. Marylyn not only began to restore the house back to its period with primitive antiques, but tackled the grounds using stacked stone walls, a stone drive, simple gardens, and a unique pergola.

Marylyn loves to integrate her primitive antiques, stone pieces, and patriotic flags into her gardens.

Gardening comes naturally to Marylyn as her last name, Garofalo, translates to "carnations". Her Italian father's gardens were the highlight for many who stopped by while on their Sunday drives in the 1950's and 60's. In fact, Marylyn continues the tradition in one regard, as she plants hundreds of flowers to create bouquets for friends who visit.

Marylyn has created a peaceful enclosed pergola at one side of the backyard with flags and lattice panels giving the area a feel of privacy. The stone figures represent the four seasons and were molded from those from an 1800's Connecticut garden.

A sign with the name of her shop, Strictly Country, is tucked in the corner of the open porch at the back of the house. Marylyn, an antique dealer for over 30 years, sells her pieces by appointment only. She may be contacted at mgk110@yahoo.com.

Chapter 15

The Lindberg/Nelson Gardens

Nancy Lindberg and Dan Nelson purchased their 1850's home in Norfolk, Massachusetts, 13 years ago . . . and were thanked profusely by the neighbors for doing so. Although the house was in total disrepair, Nancy was drawn to the property by the huge trees, old plantings, and the woods surrounding the property. Nancy has collected antiques for over 30 years and likes to integrate primitive pieces into her flower beds, although she admits she prefers the perennials to remain center stage.

Nancy loves to use old chairs and is drawn to the springs found in old baby cribs. She loves the form the springs provide as a trellis for her climbing plants and vines.

Nancy's shade beds are located where the horse corrals formerly stood.

The potting shed is a former chicken coop and was rescued from a farm up the street; it was about to be torn down. The owner left the shed on Nancy and Dan's front lawn, and they used logs to move it to the back of the house.

The whimsical angel hanging on the potting shed door was created by a friend.

Nancy's shop, Nothings New, is located at 224 Dedham Street (Rt. 1A), Norfolk, Massachusetts. She is open Tuesday-Sunday 10-5. The shop's phone number is 508-384-7666. Nancy can also be found on Facebook by searching Nothings New Norfolk.

Chapter 16

The Davidian Gardens

I'm often reminded of the small world we live in and how closely knit we collectors of country are. It has happened many times that as I'm photographing a home, the homeowner will say something like, "I used to own your dining room table" . . . or the yarn winder I photographed in a home in Massachusetts I learned later belonged to a woman in Kentucky. A similar instance occurred with the home of Betty and Peter Davidian of East Dennis, Massachusetts. Betty and Peter moved to the Cape in 2008 from a home featured in my previous book, *Holidays at a Country Home*. Their house in East Dennis is a half cape, the oldest section of which was built in 1723 by Deacon Daniel Hall. Betty and Peter have had their business, davidian-americana, for over 40 years specializing in early country smalls and furniture with original paint or surface. In addition to selling by appointment, they maintain a booth and case at the Sandwich Antique Center on Rt. 6A in Sandwich, Massachusetts; the interior of their home will be featured in a future book.

When Betty and Peter moved to the property, they filled a gap in the stone walls that surround the entire property with the trellis, seen right. Betty suspects there had been a trellis previously in the same spot, as there were trumpet vines on each side of the gap.

Betty reported that it has taken her a few years to figure out what perennials thrive on the Cape. She has had good luck with spring bulbs which border the driveway up to the house.

Peter and Betty built the addition off the back of the house to create a secluded area for a patio.

Betty wanted the patio, while Peter preferred a koi pond; they compromised by locating the koi pond immediately beyond the patio. A Japanese cut leaf tree adds a deep red contrast against the yellow moonbeam coreopsis.

In the summer, flowers and shrubs grow tall enough that the pond is not only hidden from large birds but also shaded from the intense sun and heat.

A dove cote is tucked in the garden behind a bee skep house that Peter made.

Betty has found that hydrangeas thrive in the yard; she has used them together with roses to line a bed on the side of the house.

Beautiful wisteria cascades and covers the side of the detached garage.

davidian-americana is located at 311 Scargo Hill Road, South Dennis, Massachusetts, 02660.

For an appointment, please call 508-385-1341.

Chapter 17

❧ ✿ ❧

The Aker Gardens

Now that Roger Aker is semi-retired, he has time to spend enjoying what he likes to do best . . . gardening and building. Roger's wife Judy doesn't mind a bit that Roger takes care of the extensive vegetable gardens-and she tends to her flowers. The Akers live in Aitkin, Minnesota, in the home they built 12 years ago. Both natives of Minnesota, they take full advantage of a short growing season. Judy enjoys collecting antiques and gravitates more toward primitives as opposed to the "up north" décor she refers to as being common in their area.

Roger built almost all the birdhouses in Judy's flower beds and two large sheds in the back yard.

Judy likes to mix color combinations; alongside the deck her red, white, and blue garden proves challenging to coax all the flowers to bloom at the same time.

Each year, Judy identifies one large bed which she separates and moves around. Recently, she blended the pink phlox and white lilies.

Roger built the wishing well and the small bench planter filled with impatiens.

When Roger and Judy purchased the property, it was entirely wooded. They elected to leave a large portion shaded and were thrilled to discover that they have numerous wildflowers such as trillium, Indian moccasins, and lady slippers, the state flower, growing under the trees. Interestingly, Indian moccasin flowers take 18 years to grow from seed to plant.

Judy and Roger found the large piece of farm equipment, a potato picker, at an auction.

Roger and Judy are members of a horticultural club which they enjoy immensely. Through the club and its members, they have learned a great deal about plants and have become involved in community beautification projects . . . when they're not working in their own yard.

W hat better place for a country garden than one surrounding an 1810 Pennsylvania stone house with a 1750's log cabin addition. Such is the good fortune of Ed and Diane Windle of Gum Tree, Pennsylvania, who restored their stone home in 1982 and then moved the log house onto the picturesque property in 1986.

You may remember the interior of the home which was featured in my previous book, *The Warmth of Home*.

The Windle's welcoming front porch is filled with primitive pieces, a prelude to the interior filled with country furniture and smalls, most of which are for sale. Diane and Ed's business, *Log Cabin Antiques*, draws customers from throughout the country seeking country pieces with old and original paint.

Diane uses a variety of containers to hold her annuals.

A gated area shown below on the side of the house along the driveway encapsulates a secluded space with a meandering stone path.

An in-ground swimming pool at the back of the house is banked with flower beds and primitive accents, while the pool deck features scattered pots of annuals and old weathered birdhouses.

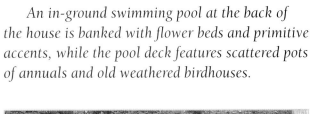

Even an old outhouse provides a tranquil and appealing visual.

Diane can be reached by phone at 610-857-3416 or 484-459-7817, and suggests a visitor call ahead. Her email address is windles_lc_antiques@hotmail.com.

Chapter 19

⌒ ✵ ⌒

The Burnett Gardens

During the last 18 years, Mike and Barbara Burnett have transformed not only their large 14 room circa 1850's colonial in Madison, Indiana, into a warm home but have managed to plant the extensive gardens throughout the property. Despite the fact that Mike has a full-time job as a VP with Madison Hospital, he still manages to enjoy "his" log cabin in the back yard and his hobby of collecting frontier items such as arrow heads and bear skin rugs. Barbara loves to garden and collect antiques, which is evident in the number of primitive accents she has added to the gardens and the variety of vignettes she has created. The log portion of their home dates to the 1700's and provides an ideal backdrop for Mike and Barbara's painted pieces.

The stone house in back dates to the 1830's. Barbara and Mike suspect that at one time the property may have been a gristmill, as they have unearthed numerous grinding stones as they developed their garden beds.

Mike built all the fences and pergolas with wood from the property.

When Mike and Barbara purchased the property, none of the 11 acres was cleared. The log cabin shown left is just one of the three they have moved and reconstructed.
In his cabin, Mike keeps a combination workshop and frontier room, while Barbara uses her cabin as a potting shed and garden room. The interior of their home was featured in my previous book, Back Home–Simply Country.

Chapter 20

The Littiken Gardens

Bob and Candace Littiken built their Hebron, Indiana home in 2001 and did much of the work themselves. The interior of their home was featured in a previous book, *A Touch of Country*. Bob admits that the gardens developed after a few trips to Colonial Williamsburg in Virginia; Bob and Candace knew they wanted a "door" garden similar to those in Virginia. Today they grow over 30 different herbs which they trade or sell to local restaurants.

Their gardens reflect their interest in country antiques which they have integrated wherever possible.

Bob and Candace created a "high rise apartment" living space with an old apple ladder and primitive birdhouses. A left-over from the days when Bob collected early garage pieces is tucked in with the hostas.

Bob and Candace use the half-barrel planter to store their hose out of sight without compromising the country setting.

Bob and Candace created an interesting backdrop in the shaded beds with the use of an old window.

Bob refers to the gate shown below, which he created using an old door, as "The gate to nowhere".

Chapter 21

The Przystas/Chojnowski Gardens

In 1997, anxious to leave his three-family house in Worcester, Massachusetts, and find a more rural, tranquil setting, Lou Przystas had been looking for lakefront property for almost a year when his realtor called and said he absolutely must come quickly to see a property on Pine Island Point which was coming on the market. Lou couldn't believe his eyes when he set foot on the property! He had to take the word of the realtor that there was a lake because the brush and trees were so thick water was not visible. The property had a leaking cesspool and oil tank, a flooded basement, and was littered with cigarette butts, broken glass, old tires, bed springs, and more. The realtor urged Lou to make an offer with a small down payment, which he did. After meeting with a town inspector and learning that the home contained lead paint, Lou also had to deal with the electrical, plumbing, and heating systems in need of repair. He then asked for his deposit back but was talked into thinking it over during the weekend.

He was torn as to what to do and felt strongly that he needed some kind of sign to help with the decision. While spending some time with friends along a river in Western Massachusetts, he drifted off to sleep on a large rock; he awoke to see a man with white hair and a white beard walking by. The man said hello and then declared that Lou had the best rock on the lake . . . and continued walking. At that point, Lou rose to look for the man, but was unable to locate him. Lou realized that this was the sign he needed–and he went ahead and purchased the property–determined to do whatever it took to make it his home.

Lou spent nine months with the Conservation Commission, Board of Health, and DEP getting permits, removing oil soaked soil, cleaning up the basement, house, and yard. The house at the time was a cottage and, in fact, was not the first house built on the property; the cottage was built over a fishing shack because state law prohibited the building of any additional structures and the previous owner wanted to take advantage of the existing foundation and the grandfathered distance to the water. Finally, Lou was able to spend his first night at the house, then spent exhausting days continuing to clear land and clean up the lakefront water area. Lou quickly reached the point where he didn't want to leave the lake to even go back to Worcester for his mail.

On Labor Day weekend, 2008, Lou returned to the river in Western Massachusetts where he had reached his decision to purchase the house. There he met a man named Eric who seemed to have much in common with Lou. They eventually became friends and Eric moved into the three-family house in Worcester while the new house was designed that would replace the cottage at the lake.

After endless planning sessions, the old cottage was torn down. A new septic system was approved and installed. Eventually, Lou's present home was built using the solid stone foundations of the first and second houses.

Lou leveraged plants given to him by family and friends and began to fill up the gardens which have been added to and enhanced over the last 10 years. He purchased a boat which can be seen at the dock.

A large planter with a hole in the bottom and rope for absorbing water sits off-shore and visually integrates the land and water.

Lou was intent on saving the large rock in the side yard, even though its location was perfect for the septic system. Lou refers to this rock now as "the best rock".

Lou's story has a happy ending! He discovered that Eric and he shared many common interests, including gardening. They've been partners now for 14 years!

The "simply country" book series

by Judy Condon

Country on a Shoestring
- 33 tips on how to decorate on a shoestring

Of Hearth and Home
- mantels, old painted pieces, signs and primitives

A Simpler Time
- log homes, bedrooms, kitchens, dining rooms, folk art and stencils

Country Decorating for All Seasons
- holiday doors, porches, mantels, trees, vignettes; summer gardens, and fall decorating

As Time Goes By
- The Keeping Room; boxes, baskets and bowls; The Privy; Hallways and Small Ways; The Guest Room

Country at Heart
- The Tavern Room; early looms, dolls and bears; The Gathering Room; a kitchen aged to perfection; country gardens

Welcome Home
- Over 350 photographs from 2 Connecticut homes and 5 Ohio homes.

Home Again
- A house tour book featuring 1 Maine home and 7 Ohio homes including a never before photographed Shaker collection.

The Warmth of Home
- 3 Massachusetts homes, 1 Pennsylvania home, 3 Ohio homes, 1 New York home and 1 Delaware home

The Country Home
- 6 Ohio homes, 2 Massachusetts homes, and 1 New Hampshire home

The "simply country" book series
(continued)

The Comfort of Home
- Over 325 color photographs showing a Massachusetts and Ohio home of two exceptional collectors. A Maine home; three Massachusetts homes, one of which is in the city.

Simple Greens – Simply Country
- Over 400 color photographs of country homes decorated for the holidays. Also a chapter on "how to make a country bed" and the recipe for the large decorative gingerbread boys and pantry cakes.

The Country Life
- The home of antique dealer, Marjorie Staufer of Ohio and Colette Donovan of Massachusetts is featured, as well as 4 other Massachusetts homes, a Maine home, a New Hampshire home and a Connecticut home of children's book author, Mark Kimball Moulton.

Simply Country Gardens
- Over 500 color photographs of "just country gardens" from twenty-three homes.

The Spirit of Country
- A house tour format book featuring homes in Virginia, Maine, Connecticut, Indiana, Ohio, Massachusetts, New Hampshire and Kentucky.

The Joy of Country
- Over 400 pictures of homes in Wisconsin, Upstate New York, Ohio, a Connecticut 18thC home, a doublewide in Delaware, 5 Massachusetts homes, a Pennsylvania home and a Maryland home converted from a 19thC granary.

Holidays at a Country Home
- The third holiday book in the series consists of over 500 color photographs of 13 decorated homes and a Condon traditional secret recipe!

A Touch of Country
- *A Touch of Country* features 8 homes. A unique collection of stoneware and weathervanes is included in one home; primitive settings and collections of early paint are highlights. Rug hookers will love one of the chapters and the avid antique collector will marvel over a Maine home!

Back Home-Simply Country
- The renovated 19thC New England cape of Judy and Jeff Condon is featured along with eight other country homes.